100 Questions and Answers About Latter-day Saints

Michigan State University School of Journalism

Front Edge Publishing

To learn more about this book and its author, please visit
https://news.jrn.msu.edu/culturalcompetence/

Cover design and illustration by Rick Nease
www.RickNeaseArt.com

Published by Front Edge Publishing
42807 Ford Road, Suite 234
Canton, MI

Front Edge Publishing books are available for discount bulk purchases for
events, corporate use and small groups. Special editions, including books
with corporate logos, personalized covers and customized interiors are
available for purchase. For more information, contact Front Edge Publishing
at info@FrontEdgePublishing.com

Contents

Acknowledgments

Bias Busters guides traditionally start with a group photo of the students who produce them. In 2020, with the outbreak of the COVID-19 pandemic, all classes at Michigan State University went online. That made our traditional photo of the authors impossible. The students, however, who adapted to all kinds of other changes, also adapted the tradition to Zoom. Here they are in their final Zoom class. From left, top row: Ally Telfor, Helen Korneffel and Alaina Agnello. Second row: Paige Geroux, Adrian Kresnak and Rachel Barry. Third row: Foster Wells, Xing Gao and Karly Graham. Fourth row: Chloe Peter and Lucas Day. Not pictured: Mackenzie Dent, Yiyang Li and Hakeem Weatherspoon.

This guide was blessed with a number of dedicated allies who taught the authors, critiqued drafts and hosted them at the Lansing Institute near the Michigan State campus. The Stoddard Student Living Center, one of the church's few such residences, is right across the street from campus. Many other people agreed to be interviewed, including a member of the Romney family.

Our allies included:

Sterling Brennan, president of the Lansing Mission, who explained the Mission Program and the selection process.

Eric and **Laura Hunter**, ecclesiastical leaders of the Lansing, Michigan Student Congregation. They were our first guests. Eric, associate dean for research in the MSU College of Communication Arts and Sciences, offered advice about the class months in advance

Michele Steed, public affairs/communication director for the central and northern Michigan area covering approximately 40 congregations. She, too, advised on the setup of the course, visited our class and met with us at the institute.

Nicholas W. Gentile, Lansing Institute director and coordinator for Seminaries and Institutes of Religion and an excellent teacher. He opened his classes to us and came to our classroom with a slide presentation on navigating church resources and a suitcase full of reference books, several of which appear in the resources section at the end of the guide.

Kirk Leifson, lifelong church member who is public affairs/communication director for the church in Southeast Michigan, which incorporates 40 congregations. He and **Karin Dains** advised the instructor months before the class began and reviewed a draft of the manuscript.

David Olsen, a member of the Bloomfield Hills, Michigan, stake presidency. He reviewed a draft of the guide.

Barb Miller, administrative assistant in the MSU College of Communication Arts and Sciences' Knight Center for Environmental Journalism. She made valuable connections for us.

Jana Riess, a senior columnist for Religion News Service and author of several books including "The Next Mormons: How Millennials Are Changing the LDS Church." She provided advice on the manuscript.

Richard Epps, MSU School of Journalism web and publication design professor. He coordinated graphics by students, whose names are on their contributions.

Finally, we wish to thank MSU School of Journalism professor and director **Dr. Tim P. Vos** for his support of this series.

Foreword

By Joel Campbell

Krister Stendahl, the Swedish theologian and former dean of the Harvard University School of Divinity, on several occasions spelled out his three rules for religious engagement.

1. "Let the 'other' define themselves. Don't think you know the other without listening." To not talk to those who are believers of a faith and relying on inaccurate information from critics is "bearing false witness," Stendahl said.

2. "Compare equal to equal, not my positive qualities to the negative ones of the other."

3. Find beauty in the other so as to develop "holy envy."

As a life-long Latter-day Saint and a career journalist and journalism educator, I find Stendahl's advice a good guide for anyone — even someone unaffiliated with a faith — to understand another's beliefs. This book allows Latter-day Saints to define themselves while readers "listen" to the 100 questions. The Q and A format presents facts in a non-judgmental and non-comparative way to avoid the "positive to negative" comparisons. It also leaves room for some "holy envy."

Professor Joe Grimm and his students at Michigan State complement Stendahl's guidelines with their production of

"100 Questions and Answers About Latter-day Saints." Like other guides in the Bias Busters series, this one is a great way to better understand the nuances of faith traditions. The information is well researched, balanced and documented and vetted by those who operate inside both the culture and ecclesiastical structure of the church. Of course, this guide gets even more personal because it's about my family's faith for five generations, The Church of Jesus Christ of Latter-day Saints.

Discussion questions at the end of the guide will spark authentic conversations and new insights. These questions allow anyone with an open mind to take a journey from an interfaith or no-faith perspective into the lives of people deeply committed to their faith, doctrines, and a Christian walk of life.

In the end, I hope those who use this book to "listen" a little bit better and learn a little more about my often misunderstood faith tradition may also discover some common ties to their own experience. And possibly there might arise some "holy envy" and respect — something the world could use a lot more of.

Dr. Joel Campbell is an associate professor in journalism in the Brigham Young University Department of Communications. He holds a master's degree in journalism from Ohio State University. He worked for nearly 20 years as a reporter and editor for newspapers in Salt Lake City. He is active in the Association of Educators in Journalism and Media Communication's Religion and Media Interest Group. Campbell also critiqued a draft of this guide.

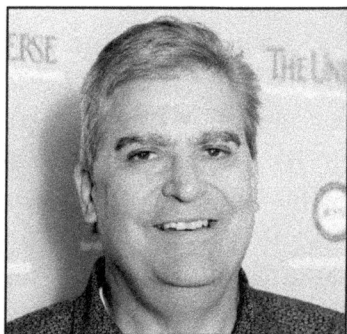

Introduction

By Karin Dains

As The Church of Jesus Christ of Latter-day Saints begins its third century, we continue to look forward with optimism and faith. Although the world now suffers great challenges, our values remain the same: faith in the Lord Jesus Christ; faith in the strength and love of families; belief in ongoing revelation; trust in our Heavenly Father's plan for each of us.

We will continue to reach out to others through missionary efforts, through involvement with interfaith organizations, and through active engagement with those who promote equality and freedom for all, regardless of faith or race. In times of trial, rancor and enmity, we believe that solutions can be found by turning to God. As Russell M. Nelson, the president of The Church of Jesus Christ of Latter-day Saints, has said: "We can turn to Him for healing of our hearts, for strength where we are weak, and for help to do things we simply cannot do on our own."

We believe that Heavenly Father has created and loves all His children and that we are all His sons and daughters regardless of our birth circumstances. During a speech at the NAACP Convention in Detroit in July of 2019, President Nelson said: "We are all connected, and we have a God-given responsibility to make life better for those around us. We don't have to be alike or look alike to have love for each other.

We don't even have to agree with each other to love each other." We believe one of our key responsibilities is to learn about and to appreciate one another's differences.

The church's 12th Article of Faith reads: "We claim the privilege of worshiping Almighty God according to the dictates of our own conscience, and allow all men the same privilege, let them worship how, where, or what they may." At a time of universal unrest, that guideline becomes even more sacred. We embrace and advocate freedom of religion and the ability to worship according to the dictates of our consciences. We stand together with people of all faiths in defending this sacred right.

As you learn about our faith, we want you to know that we welcome your questions. Not only can they help your learning process, but they will enable us to understand your viewpoint and to hopefully create friendships and increase understanding. We wish Heavenly Father's and Jesus Christ's blessings to be with everyone and pray for peace and health for all.

This is not an official statement of The Church of Jesus Christ of Latter-day Saints.

Karin Dains made the 150-mile round-trip from the church's stake in Bloomfield Hills, Michigan, where she is public affairs representative for 11 congregations, to speak to the Bias Busters class. She also reviewed a draft. Dains is a member of the boards of directors of the InterFaith Leadership Council of Metropolitan Detroit and WISDOM, Women's Interfaith Solutions for Dialogue and Outreach in Metro Detroit.

Preface

In 2020, the 200th anniversary of its origin, The Church of Jesus Christ of Latter-day Saints made major clarifications in its identity and mission. These included the reassertion of its name, a new General Handbook, and changes in several policies and practices.

A global, highly organized church founded in the United States, it has labored under stereotypes from the beginning.

Although it posts information on one of the world's largest faith-based websites, outsiders still regard it as secretive. They misunderstand or ridicule its beliefs and motives and have been known to shun church members.

Given the church's bicentennial changes and its prominence in the 2020 election, the Michigan State University School of Journalism decided to publish this guide.

We in no way pretend to do the job the church does in telling its own story. The church is excellent at this. Rather, we hope to help people looking for an introduction to the church and answers to some of their basic, everyday questions. We made this guide to be a gateway.

Perhaps a co-worker or neighbor is a Latter-day Saint or you read something that left you with questions. We hope these answers will ease your concerns about asking a question in the wrong way or feeling embarrassed about asking.

We hope people will read this concise guide, gain some confidence and then turn to church members they know or the resources at the end of the guide.

As we have found in this series of some 20 cultural competence guides, people are much more alike than they are different. Also, we have seen tremendous variety within groups, so it helps to talk to several members.

Joe Grimm
Series editor
School of Journalism
Michigan State University

About the Cover

Perhaps you noticed the honeycomb pattern on our cover. Surely, some church members picked up on that right away.

The honeycomb is a nod to a motif that has been used by many communities, including The Church of Jesus Christ of Latter-day Saints. Val Brinkerhoff, associate professor of photography in the Department of Visual Arts at Brigham Young University, made a study of the symbol's use starting in the Old Testament. Brinkerhoff wrote that bees appeared in the Book of Mormon under the name deseret.

Beehives symbolized the promised land, the kingdom of God. In the Utah Territory in 1848, church members called their new home Deseret and wanted that for the name of a new state. The symbol appeared in architecture, on coins and in publications, but the name did not fly when Utah was admitted to the union in 1896.

However, the influence stuck. Utah is known today as the Beehive State. Its flag and seal bear a beehive, and so do its highway signs. The symbol has lost some of its religious significance and is now taken to mean industry,

a hard-working community or cooperation. The Deseret News, owned by a Church of Jesus Christ of Latter-day Saints holding company, carries a beehive on its website and at the end of print articles.

Cover photos are courtesy of The Church of Jesus Christ of Latter-day Saints. This material is neither made, provided, approved, nor endorsed by Intellectual Reserve, Inc. or The Church of Jesus Christ of Latter-day Saints. Any content or opinions expressed, implied or included in or with the material are solely those of the owner and not those of Intellectual Reserve, Inc. or The Church of Jesus Christ of Latter-day Saints.

Identity

1 What are church members called?

There are several ways to refer to members of The Church of Jesus Christ of Latter-day Saints. They prefer "Latter-day Saints" or "members of the restored church of Jesus Christ." In this guide, we refer to them as church members or Latter-day Saints.

2 Why are members called "Saints"?

"Saint" is simply an indication that members aim to follow a life of Christ. Wm. Grant Bangerter, previously a general authority of the church, explained. He wrote, "A saint is one who follows Christ in holiness and devotion with a view fixed on eternal life."

3 The church now discourages "Mormons." Why?

References to "Mormons," "Mormonism" and "The Mormon Church" are now outdated. Church President Russell M. Nelson said a 2018 revelation prompted him to encourage members to use the full name of the church. Members believe this name was ordained by Jesus Christ. "Mormon" is acceptable in reference to the Book of Mormon or the prophet it is named for. The church discourages abbreviating its name as LDS. These style updates are meant to place the focus upon Jesus Christ. The church's new style guide is reprinted at the end of this guide.

4 What does "latter-day" mean?

Latter-day means after the church restored what it sees as the true teachings and practices of Christianity.

5 Are Latter-day Saints Christians?

Yes. They believe that Jesus Christ of the New Testament is the Son of God. They believe Jesus was crucified to atone for human sins and rose three days later. The life and teachings of Jesus are central to the church. However, Latter-day Saints differ with Protestants, Catholics and Orthodox Christians on some major points. Latter-day Saints see God as a separate being from the Son and the Holy Ghost. Other Christians typically believe in a more unified Trinity.

6 What are other differences?

Latter-day Saints believe their church, founded by Joseph Smith, reestablishes early Christian teachings as they were intended. Members follow the Bible but disagree with how some people have interpreted it. Latter-day Saints believe in an open canon, meaning the teachings of the Bible can be expanded. Latter-day Saints follow the Old and New Testaments as well as some of their own sacred texts.

7 Do Latter-day Saints evangelize?

More than 60,000 church missionaries around the world spread its message and welcome new members. Proselytizing has been a key part of The Church of Jesus Christ of Latter-day Saints since its founding. Because they are Christians and evangelize, members of the church are sometimes confused with evangelical Christians. However, they differ on several key matters of faith.

8 Why are some men called elders and some women called sisters?

The title "elder" does not signify age. It is given to members of the Melchizedek priesthood, male missionaries and senior church leaders. Female missionaries and other women in the church are called "sister." The titles are typically used in connection with their work and could be compared to courtesy titles in the secular world.

9 What are core church values?

Core beliefs are in the Thirteen Articles of Faith. These include belief in God, Jesus and the Holy Ghost, atonement for sins and Jesus' eventual return to Earth. Members place high importance on family, following the rule of law and living a pure life. The Thirteenth Article says, "We believe in being honest, true, chaste, benevolent, virtuous, and in doing good to all men."

History

10 When was the church established?

In 1820, Joseph Smith was seeking wisdom about the nature of God and faith when he said God called him. Smith wrote that he had a vision while praying in the woods. Smith wrote that God the Father and Jesus Christ appeared and told him modern Christianity had strayed from its roots. Smith reported more visions of an angel named Moroni over the next 10 years. On Sept. 21, 1823, The angel showed Smith a book of golden plates engraved by Moroni's father, the prophet Mormon. It recounted the experiences of biblical inhabitants of the Americas soon after the Resurrection. Smith translated these into English as the Book of Mormon. The church was organized in Fayette Township, New York, in April 1830 as the Church of Christ. In 1838, Smith reported a revelation to change the name to The Church of Jesus Christ of Latter-day Saints.

11 Who was Joseph Smith?

Early Life

Smith was born in 1805 into a poor farming family in Vermont headed by Joseph Smith Sr. His parents raised him as a Christian and moved to upstate New York. Smith said he was lightly educated in reading, writing and "the ground rules of arithmetic."

Religious Life

At the time of his first vision, Smith was 14. During the next 10 years, he divided time between working different jobs and translating the plates. The area was being swept by Protestant Christian revivals at the time. Smith was criticized for his contrary views and story of the golden plates. Smith wrote, "my telling the story had excited a great deal of prejudice against me among professors of religion, and was the cause of great persecution, which continued to increase … men of high standing would take notice sufficient to excite the public mind against me, and create a bitter persecution."

Family Life

Smith married Emma Hale in 1827. Together, they had nine biological children, five of whom lived to adulthood, and adopted two. Additionally, Smith engaged in the practice of plural marriage. It is unclear exactly how many wives Smith had. The ages of his wives ranged from 14 to 56 at the time of marriage.

12 How many people saw the golden plates?

According to church history, 13 in total. Smith showed the plates to three witnesses with the angel Moroni present. A few days later, without Moroni, Smith showed the plates to eight more men, including his father and two brothers. Moroni, without Smith, also revealed the plates to Mary Whitmer, who worked at the home where Joseph and

Emma Smith were staying. Whitmer was the final known witness.

13 Why did the church leave New York State?

Beginning in 1830, Smith wrote, he received instructions to relocate the church to Ohio. He was then directed to build Zion, the New Jerusalem, at Independence, Missouri.

14 Have there been schisms and offshoots in the church?

Yes, almost from the beginning. Today, the church uses courts and its communications to protect its identity. One of the longest running disputes was with the Community of Christ, known from 1872 to 2001 as the Reorganized Church of Jesus Christ of Latter Day Saints. Offshoots in Mexico date back to 1855. The church recently sued a small group in Canada that allows polygamy for using a variation of the church's name. The Church of Jesus Christ of Latter-day Saints has disavowed several groups that have called themselves fundamentalist sects. This includes the Fundamentalist Church of Jesus Christ of Latter-day Saints, which is separate and considered to be its own religion. The Church of Jesus Christ of Latter-day Saints is not affiliated with polygamous groups.

15 What were "the Mormon Wars"?

The name has been used for conflicts in Missouri (1838), Illinois (1844-1846) and Utah (1857-1858). The first two involved communities intent on driving out church settlements. In Missouri, members were killed and wounded, property was taken or destroyed, and the governor issued an extermination order. Shortly after the order was issued, rogue militiamen attacked a settlement at Haun's (or Hawn's) mill, killing 17 church members, some of them execution style. The state rescinded the extermination order and apologized in 1976. The church re-established itself and built a temple in Nauvoo, Illinois, in 1842. Persecution continued. A mob killed Smith and his brother Hyrum in the Carthage, Illinois, jail. Others were killed, too. Facing expulsion, the church embarked on the 1,300-mile Mormon Trail, led by Smith successor Brigham Young, to Utah. The Nauvoo temple was set on fire two years after most of the Saints had left the city. In Utah, hostilities between people in the territory and the federal government culminated in the Mountain Meadows Massacre of 1857. In it, a militia of church members killed 120 people in a wagon train of settlers.

16 Where did the church settle?

Members settled in the Salt Lake Valley. Here, Young established the church's permanent headquarters. He drew thousands of church members to the valley. They proposed a new state, to be called Deseret, a name from the Book of Mormon. Congress rejected that name, and Young served an uneasy time as governor of the newly created Utah Territory. From there, Young sent settlers throughout the West. They became part of several mountain states from Canada to Mexico. Utah became a state in 1896.

17 How are today's leaders changing the church?

The church made many changes around its 2020 bicentennial. These include renewed emphasis on the church's full name, shorter Sunday meetings, expanded mission opportunities, more home scripture studies and larger roles for young people. Women now have greater involvement in temples and annual conferences. Same-sex couples may have their children baptized. Many of the changes were led by Russell M. Nelson, a prominent heart surgeon who, in 2018, became the church's president and prophet at age 93.

18 What influence are young members having?

They are advocating for change, too. As some return from missionary service, they are moving into other service opportunities. According to a 2019 study called "The Next Mormons," Millennial members seek a larger role for women, LGBTQ inclusion and changes in church orthodoxy. Brigham Young University students have protested the university's honor code prohibitions against same-sex relationships. The church soon responded with a clarifying statement. It said, "Same-sex romantic behavior cannot lead to eternal marriage and is therefore not compatible with the principles included in the Honor Code."

Scriptures

19 What are the church's sacred texts?

The church relies on four sacred texts. They are the Bible, the Book of Mormon, the Pearl of Great Price, and Doctrine and Covenants.

20 What is the Book of Mormon?

Like the Bible, it is a testament to Jesus Christ's divinity and involvement with humankind. The book supplements the Bible in teaching that Jesus is savior to all people of the world. Members believe the Book of Mormon contains writings by prophets who led a group of people in the Americas. The book describes their spiritual history and documents Jesus' time following his resurrection.

21 Who wrote the Book of Mormon?

Members believe the book was authored by multiple prophets, compiled by the prophet Mormon and translated by Smith. Martin Harris, Smith's scribe, showed the first 116 pages of the translation to friends and relatives and lost the document. Because of this, Smith temporarily lost the gift to translate. After repenting, Smith regained this ability and resumed translating. Almost the entire Book of Mormon was translated over three months in 1829.

Views about human evolution among Latter-day Saints

% of Latter-day Saints who say humans...

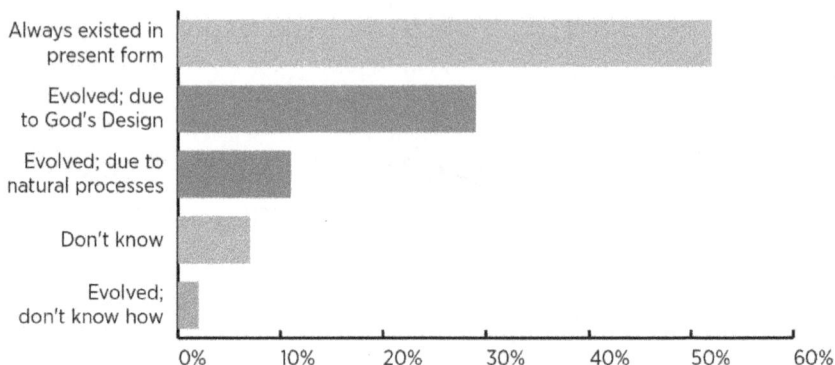

Always existed in present form	
Evolved; due to God's Design	
Evolved; due to natural processes	
Don't know	
Evolved; don't know how	

0%   10%   20%   30%   40%   50%   60%

Source: Pew Research Center   Graphic by Naomi Hatch

22 How are the Book of Mormon and the Bible related?

Believers say the book is a second testament of Jesus Christ's divinity. Both books follow God's interactions with people but overlap. The Bible focuses on Israel and Egypt, while the Book of Mormon focuses on Jesus' appearance in the Americas. The books share inspiration, guidance and lessons. The Book of Mormon corroborates the teachings of the Bible and God.

23 Which version of the Bible is preferred?

Members believe that correctly translated Bibles contain the word of God. The King James Version was the standard translation at the time of the church's founding and is preferred for English-speaking members. The best measure of any biblical translation is to compare it with the Book of Mormon and modern-day revelations.

24 What are the Pearl of Great Price and Doctrine and Covenants?

The Pearl of Great Price, published in 1851, contains information now in the church's Doctrine and Covenants. Editions published since 1902 have Smith's translations of various scriptures. They include the books of Moses and Abraham. Those describe creation, the purpose of life, humans' lives before what is commonly referred to as original sin, and the last days. In the Pearl of Great Price, Smith described his own story. It also includes the Articles of Faith.

Beliefs

25 Who do Latter-day Saints believe Jesus is?

They believe Jesus is literally the flesh-and-blood son of God the Eternal Father. Jesus has the perfection, attributes and glory of the Father. Jesus created the world under the direction of God and is Jehovah, the God of the Old Testament. Saints believe Jesus was crucified, died and rose in flesh and blood to atone for the sins of all people. They believe that God, Jesus and the Holy Spirit are three different entities who work in concert as one godhead.

26 Who is the Holy Spirit?

The church says the Holy Spirit, or Holy Ghost, works with God and Jesus. The Holy Spirit is called a guide, comforter, teacher and character builder. He manifests himself in good thoughts and ideas and in peaceful feelings.

27 Do members believe in the Trinity?

They do not believe, as some churches teach, in a three-in-one unified embodiment of the trinity. They believe each has his own purpose in our lives, and that they work together as three separate entities: God the Father, his son

Jesus Christ, and the Holy Spirit. They believe that they are unified but maintain individual personalities. God the Father is the father of all humankind's spirits. Jesus Christ advocates for humankind. The Holy Spirit guides, comforts and influences mankind.

28 What is the Restoration?

The church says a restoration of God's truth was needed because the killing of Jesus and his original apostles meant the presiding priesthood authority was lost. No one had authority to confer the Holy Ghost or perform saving ordinances. Jesus' doctrine and ordinances were then changed to conform to worldly philosophies. Scriptures were rewritten. New creeds, or statements of belief, based on false doctrine were created. God told Smith that

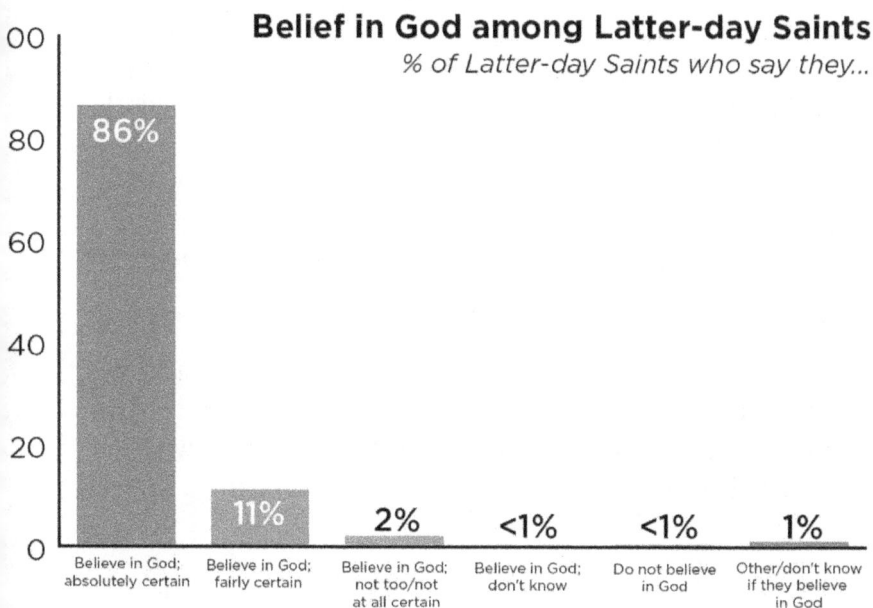

Belief in God among Latter-day Saints

% of Latter-day Saints who say they...

Category	%
Believe in God; absolutely certain	86%
Believe in God; fairly certain	11%
Believe in God; not too/not at all certain	2%
Believe in God; don't know	<1%
Do not believe in God	<1%
Other/don't know if they believe in God	1%

Source: Pew Research Center   Graphic by Allia McDowell

Christian churches were following "incorrect doctrines and that none of them was acknowledged of God as His Church and kingdom." This threw the world into a long period of apostasy, or spiritual darkness. These had occurred before. With widespread apostasy, God withdraws priesthood authority to teach and administer the ordinances of the Gospel. Smith was called to restore the original teachings. That included the return of earthly priesthood power, spiritual gifts and revelation. Members believe this Restoration is led by the living prophet of the church, who heads its presidency. Members believe that reformers and others made significant sacrifices to pave the way for a restoration.

29 Are there prophets today?

Latter-day Saints believe there are prophets in addition to the church's president. Prophets are divinely inspired to deliver God's message. However, the president alone also has the office to initiate changes to church doctrine and guidelines.

30 Do members believe Jesus lived in America?

They do not believe Jesus lived in America. They believe Jesus visited the Americas, as recorded in the Book of Mormon. They also believe descendants of the Jewish tribes of Israel settled in America.

31 Can non-members be saved?

Yes, Jesus was sacrificed for the sins of all and made salvation possible for everyone. However, the kingdom an individual may reach depends on words, deeds and thoughts.

32 What does the church teach about the afterlife?

The church teaches that God plans for everyone with very few exceptions to reach an eternal kingdom. Elder Quentin L. Cook explained in 2009, "Because of the atonement of Jesus Christ, all spirits blessed by birth will ultimately be resurrected, spirit and body reunited, and inherit kingdoms of glory that are superior to our existence here on Earth." While Jesus' atonement for humankind's sins means salvation, placement depends on how we live on Earth. The Doctrine and Covenants expands on Corinthians to describe three kingdoms. Most will reach one of these levels. Only a few will experience eternal darkness. Levels are:

Celestial Kingdom: The highest level, this is eternal life in the presence of God the Father and Jesus Christ. It follows a lifetime of righteousness.

Terrestrial Kingdom: Individuals experience Jesus' presence but not that of God the Father. It is reserved for those deemed less valiant in their testimony.

Telestial Kingdom: This brings neither Christ's testimony nor his Gospel. It is for those who were not righteous, did not believe in Jesus or the prophets and who were not baptized.

Outer Darkness: For a very small number of people whose lives made them unworthy of glory.

33 What holidays do Latter-day Saints celebrate?

Latter-day Saints celebrate Christmas and Easter. A holiday specific to the faith is Pioneer Day. It is on July 24 and commemorates the settlement by Brigham Young and other pioneers in Salt Lake City. Members participate in a parade. Some make a trek commemorating the early settlers' exodus West.

Church Hierarchy

34 How is the church organized?

The head of the church is Jesus Christ. It has a highly organized structure with general authorities, general officers and local leaders. It makes extensive use of councils and consensus.

35 Who leads the church on Earth?

The church is led by 15 apostles. Apostles are special witnesses of Jesus Christ called to teach and testify of him throughout the world. They are regarded as prophets and seers. The man who has been an apostle the longest is president of the church. With inspiration, the president selects two other apostles as counselors. These three are the First Presidency, the highest governing body of the Church. The other men are the Quorum of the 12. They teach and testify throughout the world and help decide matters including policy, mission work and temple building.

36 Is the president infallible?

Prophets such as the church president do not claim infallibility or maintain that everything they say is what

Jesus would say. Nor is everything they say prophetic. Smith said, "A prophet was a prophet only when he was acting as such."

37 What is the next level of authority?

This is the Presidency of the Seventy. These are seven men from the first and second quorums of the Seventy. They are called by the First Presidency. These two quorums are General Authority Seventies. They go anywhere in the world to teach church leaders, missionaries and congregations. Ten more quorums, called Area Seventies, are responsible for global areas. The term "Seventies" comes from God's instruction to Moses to take 70 elders of Israel up to the Holy Mount. Quorums of the Seventy do not have literally 70 members.

38 What is the structure at the local level?

The church is organized into regional stakes. Each stake is led by a presidency: a president with two counselors. The president is its presiding high priest. Stakes have councils of 12 high priests. The term comes from the prophet Isaiah, who compared the early church to a tent anchored by its stakes. Lay people rotate through the positions. Each stake has five to 12 congregations. Those with more than 300 people are called wards. Smaller congregations are called branches. A ward has one bishop and two counselors. A branch has a president and two counselors.

39 What is priesthood?

Priesthood is the authority to represent God and act in his name. The church says it is the only organization on Earth with priesthood authority. Two types were conveyed to Smith. The Melchizedek priesthood and its authorities, which are called keys, was restored when apostles Peter, James and John conveyed it to Smith. He received the Aaronic priesthood and its keys from John the Baptist. Priesthood keys are the authority to grant ordinances and blessings in God's name. All priests are male. The Melchizedek priesthood is the higher order, with the church president presiding. Melchizedek priesthood holders are ordained to the calling or position of "elder" or "high priest." They have authority over other church offices. Aaronic priesthood members are under the authority of bishops. All who hold positions in the Aaronic priesthood — deacons, teachers and priests — are male. They may join the Aaronic priesthood's deacons quorum in January of the year they turn 12. The teachers quorum begins in the year someone turns 14. The priests quorum starts when men turn 16. Authorities include ministering of angels, the gospel of repentance and administering with outward ordinances. These include baptism for the remission of sins.

40 What is the Relief Society?

All adult women in the church are members of the Relief Society, which the church calls the largest women's organization in the world. Smith organized the society in 1842 when the church was based in Nauvoo, Illinois. Members lead, minister, teach and help people in need.

This is how women exercise other roles in the church, as well.

41 What are general conferences?

Since its early days, The Church of Jesus Christ of Latter-day Saints has held conferences. These are opportunities for members to be together for instruction, counsel and inspiration. They help members grow in their faith. General conferences are held in Salt Lake City in April and October. They are broadcast in 90 languages and carried online. In a notable first, the First Presidency announced the Young Women and Relief Society and the priesthoods would together attend a session at the church's April 2020 conference. However, that year's COVID-19 outbreak turned the conference into a largely online event.

Ordinances and Covenants

42 What are major church ordinances or sacraments?

Ordinances are sacred, formal acts. The major ones, called saving ordinances, are essential for church members to live eternally in God's presence. They are performed by the authority of the Melchizedek priesthood. Ordinances contain covenants, or promises for this life or the future life, with God. Ordinances are also accompanied by blessings. These are saving ordinances:

Baptism

This first ordinance usually occurs at age 8. Latter-day Saints believe younger children are not accountable for understanding the covenant. Baptism is necessary for church membership and for salvation. This ordinance is experienced by total immersion in water, which symbolizes the death of a sinful life and rebirth into a spiritual one. Baptism can be performed by holders of the Aaronic priesthood. Two baptized members act as recorded witnesses to the ordinance. Recently, this privilege has been extended to women. Covenants, or promises, include pledging oneself to Jesus Christ, always remembering him and keeping his commandments. Younger children and people with mental disabilities are sinless and do not need baptism for salvation. People may be baptized at older ages, too.

Confirmation

Sometimes called "Baptism by Fire," this is the second essential ordinance and may occur any time after baptism. It signifies the Holy Ghost being conveyed through the laying on of hands by a holder of the Melchizedek priesthood. Confirmation is often accompanied by a blessing of the individual.

Temple endowment

This is one of the most sacred experiences in a Latter-day Saint's life. Preparing for it binds a person's identity with God's. Endowment brings greater knowledge of God's purposes and teachings and power to do all God wants. Accompanying gifts include divine direction and protection, hope, comfort, peace and eternal blessings. Temple endowments may be received by men or women who are at least 18. Members who are called to a mission or engaged to be married in the temple may receive this ordinance. They must be judged worthy by their bishop. This ordinance includes additional promises to commit one's life to God.

Ordination to the priesthood

The power to teach God's message is exercised through the priesthood. The Aaronic priesthood is the preparatory priesthood consisting of deacons (turning 12-13), teachers (turning 14-16) and priests (turning 16 through ordination to the Melchizedek priesthood. Offices in the Melchizedek priesthood are elder, high priest, patriarch, seventy and apostle. One must be ordained as a high priest to serve in a stake presidency, high council or bishopric. Priesthood holders preach, administer ordinances and participate in church government. They are organized into councils, called quorums. They build unity and brotherhood and teach doctrines, principles and duties. Apostles and seventies serve in quorums at the top levels of the church. Holders of the priesthood may marry. They do not wear robes or vestments particular to their office.

Marriage sealing

In the church, marriage is between one man and one woman. This is modeled by the Heavenly Father and Heavenly Mother, who are sealed for eternity. The idea of eternal sealing was lost, but with the restoration of the Gospel, marriages can again be sealed. Marriages are sealed by the proper priesthood authority, and the sealing ordinance is performed in a temple. Marriages performed outside the church are for one's lifetime only but can be sealed for eternity later for couples deemed worthy. Without sealing, spouses have no church-recognized claim on each other or their children after death. Parents and adopted children may also be sealed in a temple.

43 Are ordinances secret rites?

To respect temple sanctity, saving ordinances were typically not discussed outside religious contexts. Rumors that secret or forbidden activities happened inside temples followed. Today, the church is much more open about its ordinances. It explains them on its website and shows images. Entrance to sanctified temples is still reserved for people with a temple endowment. Among church members, the expression is that the temples are not secret, they are sacred and the saving ordinances deeply personal.

44 What are proxy ordinances?

Also called vicarious ordinances, these are performed on behalf of the deceased. These are typically ancestors who did not receive the saving ordinances while living, or who were not baptized or confirmed. Proxy ordinances are considered to be acts of great meaning and kindness that bind generations. These may be performed only in a temple. The apostle Paul taught that Jesus Christ modeled proxy baptism when he atoned for the sins of others through his resurrection. Latter-day Saints believe the deceased decide in the afterlife whether to accept baptism and confirmation by proxy.

45 What are lesser ordinances?

Besides these major acts of the priesthood authority there are other ordinances not essential for salvation. They provide blessings, comfort, guidance and encouragement. The most common one is the administration of the sacrament of the Lord's supper. "The Sacrament," as it is often called, is offered to all attending Sunday worship services. Other ordinances are the naming and blessing of children and administering with consecrated oil to the ill and afflicted.

46 What are the blessings that accompany ordinances?

Ordinance blessings are given by the authority of the Melchizedek priesthood in the name of Jesus Christ. Additionally, patriarchal blessings may be requested by individuals or their families. In these, an ordained patriarch declares the person's lineage in the house of Israel. The priest also delivers divinely inspired blessings, spiritual gifts, promises, advice and admonition.

Marriage and Family

47 What is the role of the family?

The church sees families as central to God's plan. Children are first born of the Heavenly Father and Heavenly Mother before they are born to earthly parents. The church, then, sees procreation as a "divine attribute" to be kept virtuous and pure. The church's principle of chastity, in the 13 Articles of Faith, teaches that sexual relations are appropriate only between a man and woman in marriage. It also expects fidelity of married couples.

48 How broad is the church's concept of family?

Members of the church believe strongly in keeping a close-knit family. Marriage is encouraged. Having children after marriage is valued. The idea of family transcends mortal time. Saints believe all people and their families, going back generations, can be sealed to each other and to God for eternity. Sealings keep families united even after death. Sealings usually accompany temple marriages. Church marriages can also follow a civil marriage, if a spouse converts and in the case of remarriage.

49 What is a plural marriage?

A plural marriage is between one man and two or more women. Since 1890, The Church of Jesus Christ of Latter-day Saints has maintained that marriage occurs only between one man and one woman. In the 1840s, Smith slowly instituted plural marriage, or polygamy. This was based on his study of plural marriages of biblical patriarchs including Abraham, Isaac, Jacob and Moses. Although Young also practiced polygamy, about three-quarters of adult church members did not. Two-thirds of the plural marriages were between one man and two women. Most plural families were in Utah. Women decided for themselves whether to enter a polygamous marriage, and they could divorce and remarry. The church asked some men to participate in plural marriages, and some did so on their own. Polygamy was in decline in the church and became illegal in the United States in 1882.

50 What was the purpose of plural marriage?

Smith saw plural marriages as part of the restoration of prophets and the priesthood. He also saw plural marriages as embedded with the concept of eternal marriage. The practice increased the number of children in church families and was thought to bring greater blessings. It made marriage available to more people. The church reports that plural marriages decreased wealth inequality and increased ethnic intermarriages, uniting a diverse immigrant population.

51 Is plural marriage still practiced?

The Church of Jesus Christ of Latter-day Saints has not recognized polygamy for 130 years. Groups that have taken similar names and practice polygamy are not part of this church.

52 Does the church allow divorce and remarriage?

While couples may get legally divorced, the only way to divide a sealed couple in the church is through a cancellation. Couples seeking a cancellation must first get a civil divorce. They must then be cleared by the First Presidency for a temple recommend from their bishop. If approved at this level, the cancellation goes to the church's president. After a cancellation, members may get sealed to someone else. People may not be sealed to two spouses at once. If a couple with children gets a cancellation, their children remain sealed to them, never to anyone else. The church encourages members to think deeply before choosing a spouse and explains ways to overcome marital difficulties. It encourages couples to turn to God for help during tough times.

53 Why does the church maintain genealogical records?

This helps members find ancestors so they may seal them by proxy. Records are maintained by the church's Family History Department. Genealogical records, education and software are available to members and non-members through https://FamilySearch.org.

54 What is Family Home Evening?

This is for the family to be together and practice church teachings. The purpose is to bring families closer to each other and to God. Monday nights are traditionally Family Home Evenings, so church activities and meetings are not scheduled then. Families read the Gospel, answer each other's questions about their faith and do faith-related activities. The church provides material for parents to teach their children on these nights. Families often have lessons, study scriptures, sing songs, play games and share treats.

Worship Services

55 When do members attend services?

Like many Christian religions, the church holds Sunday services. Members usually attend regularly and must attend at least once every few months to be considered active. Attending services also comes with privileges such as temple attendance and tuition subsidies at Brigham Young University, if admitted. In 2019, the length of Sunday services was shortened from three hours to two.

56 What are services like?

Regular Sunday services include two meetings. The first is a general meeting that includes the administration of the Sacrament of the Lord's Supper and sermons. The second meeting alternates between a Sunday School discussion and smaller group administrative and support meetings. For example, this is when the local members of the Relief Society get together. Children aged 3-11 attend Primary, an organization that acts as a Sunday school. The purpose of Primary, according to the "Encyclopedia of Mormonism," is to "teach children the gospel of Jesus Christ and help them learn to live it." Starting at the beginning of the year in which a child is 12, youths and adults begin Sunday School. According to the encyclopedia, Sunday School has

Attendance at religious services among Latter-day Saints

% of Latter-day Saints who attend religious services

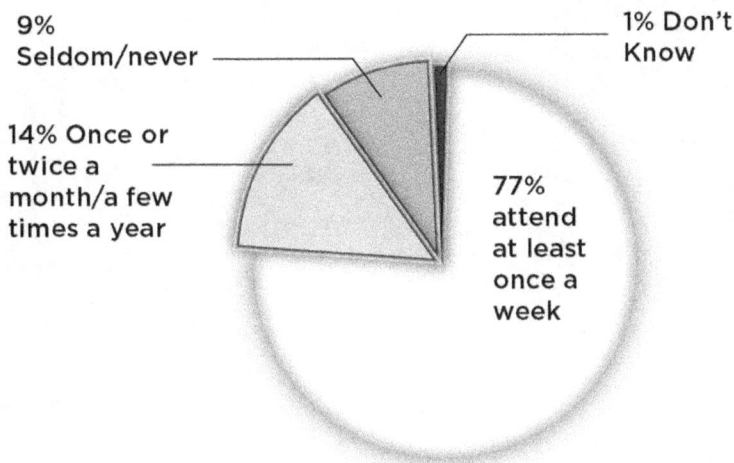

9% Seldom/never

1% Don't Know

14% Once or twice a month/a few times a year

77% attend at least once a week

Source: Pew Research Center   Graphic by Jesse Hamilton

two purposes. The first is "to strengthen individuals' and families' faith in Heavenly Father and Jesus Christ through teaching, learning, and fellowshipping." The second is to "help church members teach ... the doctrine of the kingdom at church and at home."

57 What is the difference between temples and chapels?

Temples are sacred places used for ordinances such as marriage or family sealing or proxy baptism. They are not for regular Sunday worship. That occurs in chapels, also known as meetinghouses. Chapels are also used for everyday activities for adults and children. Non-members are welcome to visit meetinghouses.

BUILDING A MORMON TEMPLE

Temples of The Church of Jesus Christ of Latter-day Saints are built using the finest materials and craftsmanship to be holy tributes to God. They are also meant to add beauty to the communities where they are constructed. Here's a look at what it takes to build one of these sacred structures.

① FUNDING

The Church sets aside funds in advance, provided by offerings from Church members, so that it can build temples without mortgages or other financing.

② SITE SELECTION

Church leaders seek guidance through prayer to identify areas where temples are most needed.

They then seek inspiration to locate a site where a temple would complement the surrounding environment and the local community.

③ DESIGN

Architects design each temple to be both energy-efficient and uniquely tailored to the local setting.

④ CONSTRUCTION

During construction, which typically lasts two to four years, only the finest materials and craftsmanship are used as a temple is meant to be a long-lasting, beautiful tribute to God.

⑤ COMPLETION

After construction is completed, a temple holds an open house for several weeks, offering free public tours inside the building.

Then it is dedicated as a holy place of worship, where Church members living the highest standards of his faith may enter. However, visitors are always welcome to tour the temple grounds.

"The temple normally will be one of the most beautiful [buildings]—if not the most beautiful building—in a community. It's natural that not just members of our church but all the members of the community generally would be very pleased to have a temple there, and they would feel it's 'our temple.'"

William R. Walker
Executive Director, Temple Department
The Church of Jesus Christ of Latter-day Saints

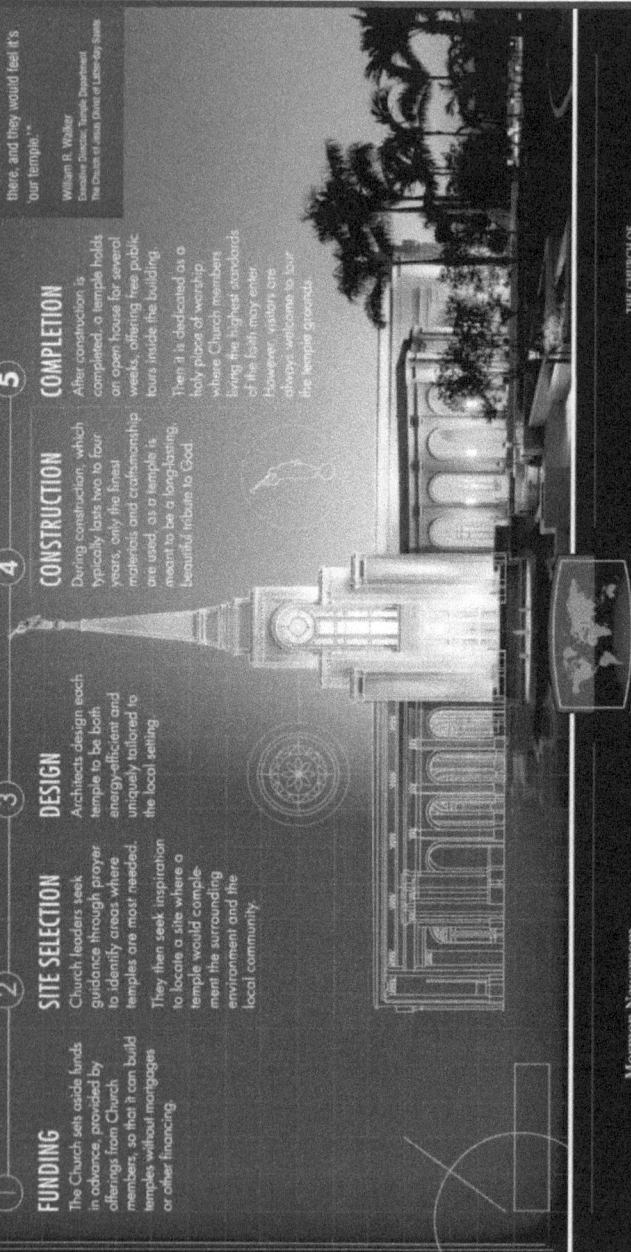

Mormon Newsroom
mormonnewsroom.org

THE CHURCH OF
JESUS CHRIST
OF LATTER-DAY SAINTS

58 How many temples are there?

The church has more than 200 temples worldwide and is building more. More than 90 are in the United States. Two dozen are in Utah.

59 May non-members enter temples?

Temples are open to non-members for a period after they have been constructed or renovated. Once a temple is dedicated, it is open only to active members approved by local leaders. Some temples have centers people may visit to learn about the church. Temple Square in Salt Lake City offers tours in 40 languages. The church welcomes thousands of non-member ancestry researchers to its archives, which are also available online.

60 What are important features of temple architecture?

There is no set style for temples, but some features are common. Temples are often made of white stone and have spires. Many temples have a spire topped by a golden statue of the angel Moroni with a trumpet. Inside the temple are rooms for ordinances, such as baptism by immersion and sealings. Favored materials are sustainable and long-lasting. Temples may have design elements that reflect the local area. In keeping with the church's value of self-reliance, temples are funded before they may be built.

Practices

61 What are sacred garments?

Latter-day Saints wear these garments under their clothes rather than for the world to see. They first receive the garments during temple endowments. They wear them to recall promises they made to God. Temple garments are white, symbolizing purity and equality among all children of God. It is disrespectful to ridicule the garments. Members of other religions including Judaism, Christianity, Islam and Sikhism also wear religious garments. Latter-day Saints believe temple garments are an outward expression of an inner commitment to follow God and his teachings.

62 What is the Word of Wisdom?

The Word of Wisdom is an evolving law of health first revealed in 1833. It offers guidance for food and substances that people should or should not put into their bodies. It encourages people to avoid alcohol, tobacco, non-herbal tea, addictive drugs and, more recently, vaping. These things are seen as harmful and addictive and interfere with members' ability to gain blessings from the Lord. Fruits, vegetables, grains and meat, on the other hand, are encouraged for health.

63 Is coffee allowed?

No. The Word of Wisdom teaches that coffee is harmful. This comes from a passage in Doctrines and Covenants that prohibits hot drinks and mind-altering substances such as caffeine. However, Brigham Young University lifted its prohibition against selling caffeinated soda on campus in September 2017. There is debate about tea.

64 Do members fast?

Members are encouraged to fast the first Sunday of every month unless their health prohibits this. Members fast for two consecutive meals. They donate the equivalent cost or more of those meals to the church as a fast offering. Funds that exceed local needs are shared regionally. Members believe fasting and praying with true intent can bring blessings for themselves and their families. Fasting is encouraged for special occasions, as well. Praying while fasting humbles members to become closer to and more like the Heavenly Father.

65 Are music and dancing prohibited?

No. Latter-day Saints are well known for their music, especially their choirs. One is The Tabernacle Choir at Temple Square, formerly known as the Mormon Tabernacle Choir. Another is BYU Vocal Point. Brigham Young University has one of the largest dance programs in the United States and is world renowned. Uplifting music and dance are encouraged. Music that glorifies violence, immorality or contains vulgar language is discouraged. Young adults regularly hold activities at church meetinghouses and dance to contemporary music. Dancing with full-body contact and suggestive or inappropriate behavior is discouraged.

66 Are tattoos and piercings allowed?

The church calls the human body a gift from God and cites scripture that says people should respect their bodies as they would a temple. The body is called home to the eternal spirit. The church cites prophets who cautioned against tattoos and excessive piercings. Some members do have tattoos.

Education

67 What are the church's educational activities?

Education plays a major role in the church. Its educational system consists of institutions that provide religious and secular education for elementary, secondary, post-secondary students and adult learners. Education is the purpose of Sunday primaries for children aged 3 to 11 and Sunday School for those aged 12 and up. Latter-day Saints see education as an eternal value that transcends mortal death. A maxim is, "The Glory of God is Intelligence."

68 What are Seminary and Institute?

These are religious education programs. Seminary is for high school students. Institute is for adults ages 18 to 30. Students study scriptures and the words of modern-day saints. Institute buildings often are adjacent to college campuses. Other locations include classrooms, homes and office buildings. More than 350,000 students are enrolled at almost 2,700 institutes around the world.

69 What is Brigham Young University?

Brigham Young University (Provo, Utah) is the largest of the four universities supported by The Church of Jesus Christ of Latter-day Saints. It is an international campus where 126 languages are spoken and 62 are taught regularly. Others are Brigham Young University-Idaho, Brigham Young University-Hawaii and Ensign College, expanded and renamed from LDS Business College in 2020. Church members are not required to attend Brigham Young University. Non-members may attend, and all students must abide by the principle-based honor code established by the Church Educational System. The church also supports an online program, https://www.byupathway.org/.

The Honor Code says:

- Be honest.
- Live a chaste and virtuous life and abstain from sexual relations outside a marriage between a man and a woman.
- Respect others and avoid profane and vulgar language.
- Obey the law and follow campus policies.
- Abstain from alcoholic beverages, tobacco, tea, coffee, vaping and substance abuse.
- Participate regularly in church services (required only of church members).
- Observe Brigham Young University's dress and grooming standards.

- Encourage others in their commitment to comply with the Honor Code.

70 What is the Perpetual Education Fund?

The church loans money from this fund to members in developing areas. It is meant to be used for education that leads to jobs. Church members and non-members contribute to the fund. Young adults seeking a loan are required to attend 12 weeks of a course called "Education for Better Work." It teaches self-reliance and helps participants explore what education best fits their skillset. It covers funding education and how to succeed in and out of school.

71 What is the typical educational level of church members?

According to a 2016 Pew Research Center study, almost one-fourth of adult Latter-day Saints had attained a high school diploma, 40% had some college and 33% had college degrees. The remaining 5% had less than a high school education.

Demographics

72 How large is the church?

The church, which began with six members in upstate New York in 1830, reported more than 16.3 million members worldwide in 2018. In the United States, there were more than 9.3 million members. Of those, about 23%, or 2.1 million, lived in Utah. That is almost two-thirds of Utah's population. While most Christian churches in the United States are shrinking, The Church of Jesus Christ of Latter-day Saints is growing, though the growth rate has slowed.

73 Do members get married younger than in other religions?

In the United States, Latter-day Saints get married younger and are more likely to marry within their religion than others. "The Next Mormons" noted that the average marriage age has risen for the whole country, including Latter-day Saints. However, they still tend to marry a little younger than others. The average age is in their early 20s. A Pew Religious Landscape Survey showed 82% of Latter-day Saints with a spouse or partner were with someone of the same religion. This was exceeded only by Hindus, 91% of whom married within their religion.

Income distribution among Latter-day Saints

% of Latter-day Saints who have a household income of...

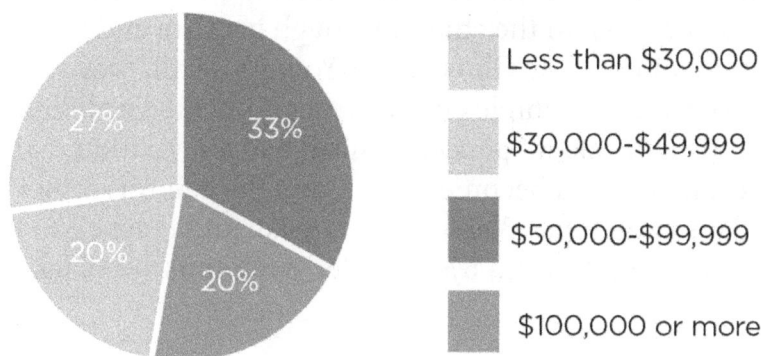

27% 33% 20% 20%

- Less than $30,000
- $30,000-$49,999
- $50,000-$99,999
- $100,000 or more

Source: Pew Research Center   Graphic by Naomi Hatch

74 Given church emphasis on children, are families larger?

Pew found that members' birth rates and family sizes are above the U.S. average. The birth average (3.4 children) and the number of children living at home (1.1) were about twice the average.

75 Does the church exclude people of color?

No. They were welcome in the early years and have been again since 1978. However, for more than 100 years in between, they were not allowed full participation. The Book of Mormon states, "black and white, bond and free, male and female; … all are alike unto God." In the early days of the church, some Black men were ordained as priests. In 1852, however, then-president Brigham

Young announced that men of African descent could no longer be ordained to the priesthood. Those who already had priesthoods retained them. Black men and women continued to join the church through baptism and received the gift of the Holy Ghost. After Young's death, they were restricted from temple endowment and sealing ordinances. In 1978, President Spencer Kimball had a revelation saying Black men could become priests, and the ban was removed. Today's church has Black, Latino, Asian and Polynesian top leaders. An estimated 6% of Latter-day Saints are Black.

Missions

76 What is missionary work?

Missionaries work in church service, visitor centers, humanitarian aid and supporting new members. According to the church website, it is designed to, "share the gospel message and help prepare family members, friends, and other acquaintances who are not Latter-day Saints to be taught by the full-time missionaries." In 2019, the church reported more than 67,000 full-time missionaries and tens of thousands of church-service missionaries. Many missionaries plan their service based on the school year. In the Northern Hemisphere, many missionaries begin their service in July, August or September.

77 Are missionary requirements different for men and women?

Men may enter a Missionary Training Center after graduating from high school or its equivalent and turning 18. Women must be at least 19. Full terms of service are two years for elders and 18 months for sisters. There are also physical health, emotional health and weight guidelines.

78 How are assignments decided?

The process begins with an application. Then, local church leaders interview potential missionaries. Once interviews are done, stake presidents send that information to the First Presidency and the Quorum of the 12, who will evaluate the various needs of missions around the world. They then pray about where to send each missionary. Based on that, assignments are made. Missionaries do not choose where they go. Assignment announcements are big news for missionaries and their families.

79 Are missionaries paid?

Missionaries receive no pay. The church encourages people to put money aside for mission work. Missionaries live on funds from themselves, their families and others. Costs have been standardized among expensive and inexpensive communities. Missionaries are advised to be thrifty, to not pack too much and to use personal funds for expenses such as clothing, buying and fixing bicycles, approved weekly phone or internet calls home, and medical expenses not paid by the mission. Missionaries receive medical care for pre-existing conditions, co-payments and normal eye or dental care.

80 Where are the missions?

The church has done outreach and missionary work throughout the world. That includes North America, Africa, Asia, Central America, Europe, South America and Oceania. Church leaders speak with leaders of foreign countries before sending missionaries.

81 How do missionaries proselytize?

Missionaries are paired or tripled with companions of the same gender. They spend the bulk of their time proselytizing. This does not necessarily mean trying to convert new members. Rather, their focus is teaching and encouraging others to read the Book of Mormon. Missionaries have a responsibility to maintain contact with converts and often continue to meet with them and reteach lessons and principles they first taught. Missionaries teach the following lessons:

- The Message of the Restoration of the Gospel of Jesus Christ
- The Plan of Salvation
- The Gospel of Jesus Christ
- The Commandments
- Laws and Ordinances

With the help of ward missionaries, the full-time missionaries encourage new members to keep the commitments in these lessons.

82 What is life as a missionary like?

Daily life for a missionary is rigorously scheduled for preparation, teaching and reflection. If necessary, there must also be time for language studies. Missionaries have a weekly preparation day, often Monday, for personal needs such as calling family, washing clothes, getting a haircut, cleaning, shopping and washing the car. They may visit tourist and historical sites, cultural centers, museums, art galleries, zoos and exhibits.

83 What is a typical daily schedule?

6:30 a.m. Wake up, pray, exercise and prepare for the day.

7:30 a.m. Breakfast

8 a.m. Personal study (the Book of Mormon, other scriptures, missionary library, etc.)

9 a.m. Companion study: prepare to teach, practice teaching, study and confirm plans for the day.

10 a.m. Begin proselytizing. An hour for lunch and additional study and an hour for dinner. Normally, dinner should be finished by 6 p.m.

9 p.m. Return to living quarters and plan next day's activities. Prepare for bed, pray.

10:30 p.m. Retire to bed.

84 Are there restrictions on missionaries' activities?

Missionaries avoid worldly entertainment including television, movie theaters, radio and internet, except to communicate with family or their mission president. Missionaries may read church-authorized books, magazines and other materials. Personal computers and electronic games are not allowed. Cellphones are under the technology section in the missionary standards handbook. It says, "Technology can be a tool to share teachings of the gospel of Jesus Christ and should be used righteously." Some members make extensive use of their phones to follow church material.

85 What do members think of the musical "The Book of Mormon"?

The Broadway show pokes fun at church missions in ways that some resent. It was written by "South Park" creators who grew up as Latter-day Saints. Church feelings about this musical, which has been performed from Broadway to Salt Lake City, are mixed. The Deseret News, a newspaper owned by a church holding company, called the show "raunchy, irrepressible, irreverent, acclaimed, denounced." However, showing its sense of humor, the church purchased an ad in the playbill for the musical. It said, "You've seen the play ... now read the book."

Money and Finances

86 Why do Latter-day Saints prioritize being debt-free?

The church encourages self-reliance and warns of dependency and debt. Latter-day Saints are not discouraged from all debt but are told to manage their finances to provide for their families without unnecessary worry. Acceptable debt includes student loans and mortgages.

87 Is the church tax-exempt?

Religious organizations are generally tax-exempt in the United States. The church is exempt from general federal taxes and, in some states, sales tax, but not from other taxes.

88 What is tithing?

A tithe is an amount of money members give to the church. To tithe means to give one-tenth, usually of one's household income. The term goes back to the

Old Testament and was adopted by early Christians. Tithing 10% of one's income is necessary to get a temple recommendation. A Latter-day Saint who does not tithe is still a church member and can participate in activities. According to the Pew Forum, 79% of Latter-day Saints tithe. Many also make fast offerings and donate to the Perpetual Education Fund, humanitarian relief and missions. Additionally, many members volunteer.

89 What are average income levels among U.S. members?

Income levels vary. According to the Pew Research Center, one-third of Latter-day Saints report annual household income between $50,000 and $99,999. One-fifth have household income of $100,000 or more. Another 20% have an income of $30,000-$49,999. The remaining 27% have an income of less than $30,000.

90 Are church leaders paid?

The church relies on the unpaid volunteer ministry of its members. This ministry is one of the Church's most defining characteristics. In thousands of local congregations or wards around the world, members voluntarily participate in callings or assignments that provide meaningful opportunities to serve. It is common for church members to spend 5-10 hours a week serving. Some callings, such as a bishop, women's Relief Society president, or stake president, may require 15-30 hours per week. Some leaders and administrators who work full time in the church receive a living allowance.

91 What is a Bishop's Storehouse?

This is a place filled with commodities provided by fast offerings and other donations. With material on hand, food and supplies can be sent on a moment's notice. They have helped in natural disasters, wars and economic crises.

92 Does the church have investments?

Yes. This issue received attention in late 2019 after a whistleblower told the U.S. Internal Revenue Service that the church had $100 billion in investments. The church responded that news stories misrepresented the truth. The church described how it helps poor and needy people around the world, builds temples, shares genealogical data, funds education and missions. The release said, "The church follows the same sound financial principles it teaches its membership. It avoids debt, lives within its budget and prepares for the future." An earlier church release on finances said, "The church maintains diversified reserves — including common stocks and bonds, interests in taxable businesses, commercial and residential real estate and agricultural properties."

Politics

93 Does the church get involved in politics?

The church is officially neutral on political parties, platforms and candidates. It encourages members to express themselves politically and to hold elected or appointed offices. Both Smith and Young held public office. Members who run are not to imply their candidacy is endorsed by the church or its leaders. The church does not let political leaders campaign in church meetings or use church buildings for campaigning. Church buildings may not be used as polling places. While usually neutral, the church will take positions on moral issues. Some have been 1981 opposition to building an MX missile system in the Utah desert, opposition to the Equal Rights Amendment, and supporting a 2008 proposition in California defining marriage as only between a man and a woman. Religious freedom is another important issue.

94 How do church members vote?

Church members tend to vote Republican. Seventy percent identify as or lean Republican, according to the Pew Research Center. Only 19% identify as Democrats, making the church the country's most Republican-leaning religion. Most Latter-day Saints voters in 2004, 2012 and 2016 voted for Bush (80%), Romney (78%), and Trump (61%). A 2018 AP VoteCast poll showed fewer than half of Latter-day Saints approved of Trump, compared to 85% of Republicans nationwide. Some church officials have been vocal opponents of Trump. As of January 2019, there were 10 church members in the U.S. Congress. Sen. Harry Reid, D-Nevada, was U.S. House majority leader from 2005 to 2017. At the state level, the Salt Lake Tribune reported that almost 90% of Utah's legislative seats in 2019 were held by church members. Eighty-one of 82 Republicans and 10 of 22 Democrats in the Legislature were members of the church.

95 Would Mitt Romney, as president, have helped his church?

When Mitt Romney ran for president as a Republican in 2016, some opponents said that. The same charge was used against John F. Kennedy, a Roman Catholic, when he ran for president as a Democrat in 1960. Romney was governor of Massachusetts for four years before becoming a U.S. senator. His father, George Romney, was governor of Michigan for six years. Both ran for president, but neither was seriously accused of pushing a religious agenda. Mitt Romney said, "I do not define my candidacy by my religion." Members of the church strongly supported Romney, with 83% of Latter-day Saints voting for him in the 2018 midterms.

Party affiliation by religious group...

% of adults who identify as...

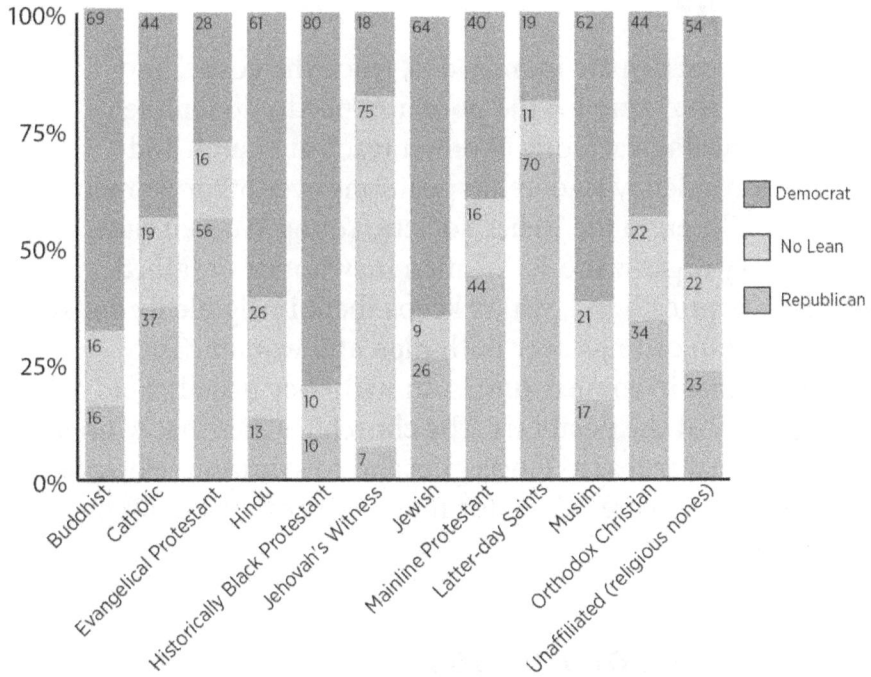

100%	69	44	28	61	80	18	64	40	19	62	44	54
75%			16			75		16	11 70			
50%	19	56		26			9 44			22	22	
25%	16 37				10 10		26		21		34	23
0%	16		13			7			17			

Legend:
- Democrat
- No Lean
- Republican

X-axis categories: Buddhist, Catholic, Evangelical Protestant, Hindu, Historically Black Protestant, Jehovah's Witness, Jewish, Mainline Protestant, Latter-day Saints, Muslim, Orthodox Christian, Unaffiliated (religious nones)

Source: Pew Research Center   Graphic by Christian Ostrowski

Social Issues

96 What is the role of women in the church?

Women participate in missions, teach the gospel and recruit. They care for the poor and needy, do temple and genealogical work. Women teach at church and hold presidency leadership positions over other women and children in the Relief Society, Young Women's and primary organizations. Women may not be ordained into the priesthood, which keeps them ineligible for most leadership callings over both men and women. They participate in some councils, though they usually hold a minority of the positions. The church teaches that women have equal access to God's gifts and to salvation. However, some women are asking for more power in the church hierarchy.

97 Can members leave the church?

Yes, members may leave the church, just as they are leaving all kinds of churches these days. Because of the close family and friendship ties in the church, it can be personally difficult. Another level of leaving is to have the church remove your name from its rolls and roster. This is usually initiated by writing a letter to church authorities

Views about same-sex marriage among Latter-day Saints

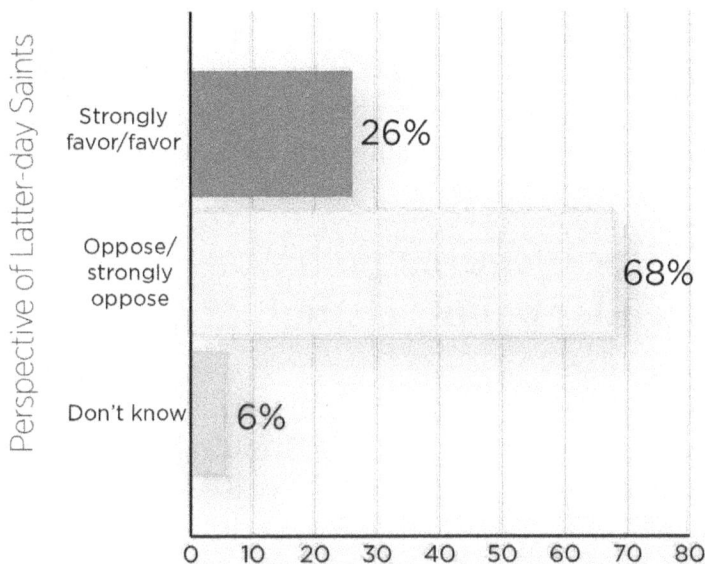

Perspective of Latter-day Saints

Strongly favor/favor	26%
Oppose/ strongly oppose	68%
Don't know	6%

0 10 20 30 40 50 60 70 80

Source: Pew Research Center   Graphic by Jesse Hamilton

within the stake where someone has been a member. Members who leave the church and wish to return will have their request considered. Returning members may have to repent for sins from when they were away. They must also give up any forbidden habits they picked up.

98 What does the church teach about same-sex attraction?

The church accepts people attracted to others of the same sex if they remain chaste. It encourages members to show people with same-sex attraction sensitivity and love. The church does not take a position on the causes of same-sex attraction. Members who are gay, lesbian or bisexual must refrain from unchaste acts, defined as sexual relations outside of marriage between a man and a woman. Members who abstain may receive callings, temple recommends, and temple ordinances. In 2019, the church removed its restriction against baptizing the children of parents who are gay, lesbian, bisexual or transgender.

99 How is church policy on transgender people changing?

The church addressed gender identity in its 2020 General Handbook. People who identify with a gender other than the sex assigned at birth are to be welcomed by other church members. They may attend services, receive the Sacrament, blessings, be baptized and call themselves by their chosen pronouns. However, people considering a medical or surgical sex transition may not be baptized or confirmed. Those who have completed sex reassignment may be baptized or confirmed if the First Presidency approves. However, access to the priesthood, temple recommends and some church callings will be limited.

100 What is the church's stance on abortion?

The church teaches that life is a gift from God, who wants his children to obtain physical bodies, be tested on Earth and have eternal life. The church opposes abortion with some exceptions. These are in cases of "forcible rape," when the mother's health would be "seriously jeopardized," incest and if the baby cannot survive birth.

Views about abortion among Latter-day Saints

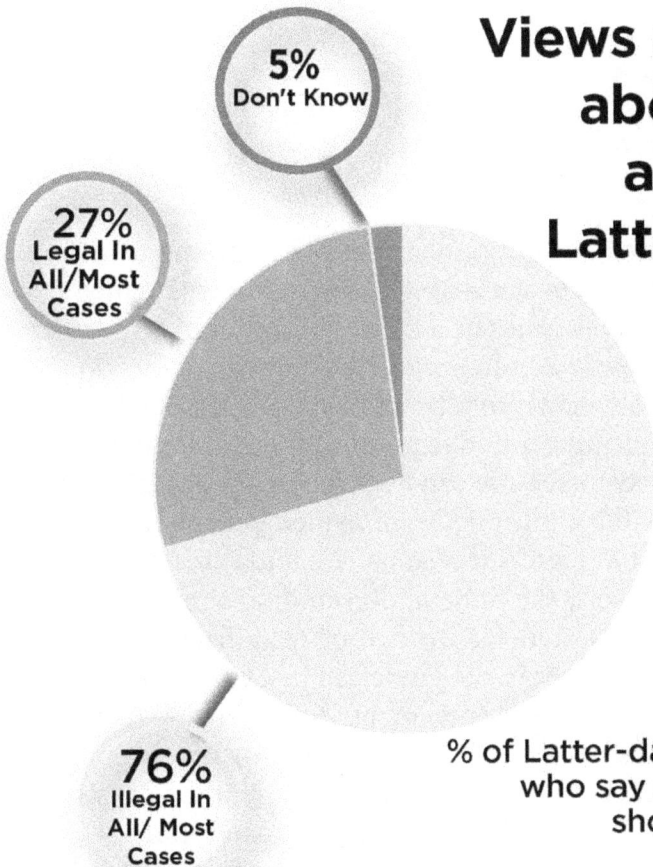

5%
Don't Know

27%
Legal In
All/Most
Cases

76%
Illegal In
All/ Most
Cases

% of Latter-day Saints
who say abortion
should be ...

Source: Pew Research Center

Graphic by Ariane Lewis

Discussion and Reflection

This guide should be only a first step. We hope you take the next one. That can be an honest conversation with a member of the church. This could be a friend, neighbor or co-worker whom you know is a church member, but with whom you have never really had a conversation about faith. We hope that can lead to greater understanding and a fuller friendship.

Another way to explore can be through a group discussion. Ideally, this will include one or more members of The Church of Jesus Christ of Latter-day Saints. We find that no two people have exactly the same understanding or experiences. For the best discussion, have everyone read this guide ahead of time. Every answer in the guide can be explored in greater depth, there might be disagreements, and there are many more questions besides. All we can do in this simple guide is answer some basic, everyday questions in hopes of raising familiarity and easing discomfort in asking questions.

Here are further questions to discuss or think about. Several come from a talk at the Poynter Institute in which the church's former managing director of public affairs, Michael Otterson, identified common stereotypes.

- Some people say Latter-day Saints are not Christians. Members do not follow all of the more than 150 creeds followed by other Christians. Saints follow some major ones, but not others, such as belief in a unified trinity. Who decides how people identify themselves? What is the power in denying a group its chosen label?

- In recent years, the church has been re-emphasizing its formal name, The Church of Jesus Christ of Latter-day Saints. The idea is to put the emphasis on Jesus, rather than on the prophet Mormon. How do terms like "Mormonism" obscure the church's identity?

- Some continue to associate the church with polygamy, although most people did not practice it and it was abolished 130 years ago. Why is that? Do shows like TLC's "Sister Wives" and HBO's "Big Love," which are about polygamist families, sustain stereotypes about the church? Should production companies do more to explain the church's disavowal of plural marriage?

- Some non-members say the church seems to be secretive and disconnected from society. This is despite a large outreach effort in person, online and through humanitarian work. What is your impression of the church? How is your impression shaped?

- The church is portrayed as a cult or as having strange practices. Does your faith group have elements that nonmembers might not understand or accept? Have you ever tried to explain them? How did that go?

- In the history section of this guide, we read that Smith said he was persecuted even as a teenage boy, soon after his first vision. That followed him right up to his assassination in Illinois. In milder ways, church members today feel discrimination. Smith seems to have attributed this treatment to skepticism and jealousy. Are there parallels for this kind of animosity today? How can we address them?

- Mission work, a rite of passage for members, has been satirized in a Broadway musical. Is this in the same vein as other musicals with religious roots such as "Nunsense" and "Fiddler on the Roof"? Do these seem to you to be the same, or different? Did you wonder what church members thought of the musical and whether it was OK to talk with them about it?

- Church members are associated with abstinence from alcohol and coffee, which is true. But some also think they abstain from music, which is not true. The Tabernacle Choir at Temple Square is known around the world. Why is there confusion? Are different churches lumped together? Why does that happen?

- Some Latter-day Saints parents have found that parents of other faiths did not want their children playing together. The other parents feared bad influences. Have you seen something like this happen? How should parents explain religious differences to their children? What interfaith lessons do children teach their parents?

- Members of The Church of Latter-day Saints have achieved success in education, business, politics, the arts and other areas. Does this help their reputation or hurt it? Why would it hurt?

- When you are approached by missionaries, what is your first thought? Does it help to remember that this is part of their faith practice?

Resources

The best place for information about The Church of Jesus Christ of Latter-day Saints is its own website. It answers questions about doctrine, history, ordinances, practices and stereotypes. Material from the site is used extensively in this guide. The site, https://churchofjesuschrist.org, is one of the most visited religious websites in the world. The site is the center of a family of sites including other church websites, life help, case studies and a YouTube channel. A related site is The Joseph Smith Papers, https://josephsmithpapers.org. Endorsed by the National Archives, it is keyword searchable and has digitized primary sources about Smith and the early days of the church.

Books

Arrington, Leonard J. Brigham Young: American Moses. New York City: Knopf; 1st edition. 1985.

Burke, Daniel and Peggy Fletcher Stack and Matt Canham. The Mormon Moment: A Religion News Service Guide. Denver: Patheos Press. Kindle edition. 2012.

Bushman, Richard Lyman. Joseph Smith: Rough Stone Rolling. New York City: Vintage reprint. 2007.

Bushman, Richard Lyman. Mormonism: A Very Short Introduction. Oxford: Oxford University Press. 2008.

The Church of Jesus Christ of Latter-day Saints. Saints: The Story of The Church of Jesus Christ in the Latter Days: Volume 1: The Standard of Truth: 1815–1846.

The Church of Jesus Christ of Latter-day Saints. Saints: The Story of The Church of Jesus Christ in the Latter Days: Volume 2: No Unhallowed Hand: 1846–1893.

Daynes, Kathryn M. More Wives Than One: Transformation of the Mormon Marriage System, 1840-1910. Champaign: University of Illinois Press. 2008.

Dew, Sheri. Insights from a Prophet's Life: Russell M. Nelson. Salt Lake City: Deseret Book. 2019.

Gee, John. An Introduction to the Book of Abraham. Salt Lake City: Deseret Book. 2017.

Givens, Terry L. By the Hand of Mormon: The American Scripture that Launched a New World Religion. Oxford: Oxford University Press. 2003.

Givens, Terry L. The Viper on the Hearth: Mormons, Myths, and the Construction of Heresy. Oxford: Oxford University Press. 2013 (updated edition).

Hales, Brian C. and Laura H. Hales. Joseph Smith's Polygamy: Toward a Better Understanding. Draper: Greg Kofford Books, Inc. 2015.

Harper, Steven C. First Vision: Memory and Mormon Origins. Oxford: Oxford University Press. 2019.

Haws, J.B. The Mormon Image in the American Mind: Fifty Years of Public Perception. Oxford: Oxford University Press. 2013.

Jackson, Kent P. From Apostasy to Restoration. Salt Lake City: Deseret Book. 2010.

MacKay, Michael Hubbard and Gerrit J. Dirkmaat. From Darkness unto Light: Joseph Smith's Translation and

Publication of the Book of Mormon. Salt Lake City: Deseret Book. 2015.

Millet, Robert L., ed. No Weapon Shall Prosper: New Light on Sensitive Issues. Salt Lake City: Deseret Book. 2011.

Ostling, Richard and Joan Ostling. Mormon America: The Power and the Promise. New York City: HarperOne. 1999, revised 2007.

Plewe, Brandon S., S. Kent Brown, Donald Q. Cannon, Richard H. Jackson, eds. Mapping Mormonism: An Atlas of Latter-day Saint History. Salt Lake City: BYU Press. 2012.

Putnam, Robert D. and David E. Campbell. American Grace: How Religion Divides and Unites Us. New York City: Simon & Schuster. 2010.

Reeve, W. Paul. Religion of a Different Color: Race and the Mormon Struggle for Whiteness. Oxford: Oxford University Press. 2015.

Riess, Jana. The Next Mormons: How Millennials Are Changing the LDS Church. Oxford: Oxford University Press. 2019.

Ulrich, Laurel Thatcher. A House Full of Females: Plural Marriage and Women's Rights in Early Mormonism, 1835-1870. New York City: Vintage. 2017.

Church Style Guidelines

Updated in 2018

The official name of the Church is The Church of Jesus Christ of Latter-day Saints. The full name was given by revelation from God to Joseph Smith in 1838.

In the first reference, the full name of the Church is preferred: "The Church of Jesus Christ of Latter-day Saints."

When a shortened reference is needed, the terms "the Church" or the "Church of Jesus Christ" are encouraged. The "restored Church of Jesus Christ" is also accurate and encouraged.

While the term "Mormon Church" has long been publicly applied to the Church as a nickname, it is not an authorized title, and the Church discourages its use. Thus, please avoid using the abbreviation "LDS" or the nickname "Mormon" as substitutes for the name of the Church, as in "Mormon Church," "LDS Church," or "Church of the Latter-day Saints."

When referring to Church members, the terms "members of The Church of Jesus Christ of Latter-day Saints," "Latter-day Saints," "members of the Church of Jesus Christ" and "members of the restored Church of Jesus Christ" are preferred. We ask that the term "Mormons" and "LDS" not be used.

"Mormon" is correctly used in proper names such as the Book of Mormon or when used as an adjective in such historical expressions as "Mormon Trail."

The term "Mormonism" is inaccurate and should not be used. When describing the combination of doctrine, culture and lifestyle unique to The Church of Jesus Christ of Latter-day Saints, the term "the restored gospel of Jesus Christ" is accurate and preferred.

When referring to people or organizations that practice polygamy, it should be stated that The Church of Jesus Christ of Latter-day Saints is not affiliated with polygamous groups.

www.ingramcontent.com/pod-product-compliance
Lightning Source LLC
Chambersburg PA
CBHW022039090426
42741CB00007B/1127